THE BONES IN YOUR BODY

LAURA LORIA

Britannica
Educational Publishing

IN ASSOCIATION WITH

ROSEN
EDUCATIONAL SERVICES

Published in 2015 by Britannica Educational Publishing (a trademark of Encyclopædia Britannica, Inc.) in association with The Rosen Publishing Group, Inc.
29 East 21st Street, New York, NY 10010

Distributed exclusively by Rosen Publishing.
To see additional Britannica Educational Publishing titles, go to rosenpublishing.com.

First Edition

Britannica Educational Publishing
J.E. Luebering: Director, Core Reference Group
Mary Rose McCudden: Editor, Britannica Student Encyclopedia

Rosen Publishing
Hope Lourie Killcoyne: Executive Editor
Jeanne Nagle: Editor
Nelson Sá: Art Director
Nicole Russo: Designer
Cindy Reiman: Photography Manager

Library of Congress Cataloging-in-Publication Data

Loria, Laura, author.
The bones in your body / Laura Loria. -- First edition.
    pages cm. -- (Let's find out! The human body)
Audience: Grades 3 to 6.
Includes bibliographical references and index.
ISBN 978-1-62275-624-7 (library bound) -- ISBN 978-1-62275-625-4 (pbk.) -- ISBN 978-1-62275-626-1 (6-pack)
1. Human skeleton--Juvenile literature. 2. Bones--Juvenile literature. 3. Bones--Diseases--Juvenile literature. I. Title.
QM101.L64 2015
612.7'5--dc23
                        2014022722

Manufactured in the United States of America

Photo Credits: Cover, interior pages background © iStockphoto.com/commotion design; pp. 4, 8, 12, 14, 15, 17, 22, 24 Encyclopædia Britannica, Inc.; p. 5 Carol Heesen/Shutterstock.com; p. 6 Dorling Kindersley/Getty Images; p. 7 Ed Reschke/Photolibrary/Getty Images; p. 9 Jupiterimages/Stockbyte/Thinkstock; p. 10 © Merriam-Webster Inc.; p. 11 racom/Shutterstock.com; p. 13 Silverjonny; p. 16 Hurst Photo/Shutterstock.com; p. 18 Fuse/Thinkstock; p. 19 Susan Leggett/Shutterstock.com; p. 20 paintings/Shutterstock.com; p. 21 Fernando Madeira/Shutterstock.com; p. 23 Blend

CONTENTS

WHY DO WE HAVE BONES?

skeletal muscle cells

biceps muscle (contracted)

triceps muscle (relaxed)

biceps muscle (relaxed)

tendon

triceps muscle (contracted)

You cannot see them, but you can feel them. You cannot stand or move without them, but you hardly ever notice them. Bones are your body's hidden frame. Bones provide a structure for your other body parts. They are connected to

Bones and muscles work together to make your body parts move.

THINK ABOUT IT

What would happen if you didn't have any bones? Would you be able to move the same ways you do now?

your muscles, and they make it possible for you to walk and run. Some bones protect the organs inside your body, such as your lungs and heart.

From the outside, a bone looks hard and still. But inside, it is always working. Bones store nutrients, or things your body needs. Bones also make blood cells.

This climber's bones keep her body stable while she plans her next move.

Bone Structure

Bones are made of calcium and other minerals, fibers of protein, and water. If you look at a bone that has been cut, you might be surprised to see that it has several layers. The outer layer of a bone is compact bone. It is firm and dense. The inner layer is spongy bone. It looks like a sponge, with many holes, but it is not soft or flexible. The holes in spongy bone are filled with bone marrow. Marrow is soft like jelly and can be red

A bone may look solid, but inside it has many holes.

or yellow. Most blood cells are created by red marrow, while fat is stored in yellow marrow.

All bones are covered with a membrane, or skin. The membrane contains nerves and blood vessels that are attached to the bone. The blood vessels carry nutrients to the bone. They also carry blood cells from the bone to the rest of the body.

COMPARE AND CONTRAST

How is the inside of a bone different from the outside?

HOW ARE BONES CONNECTED?

 bone

 cartilage

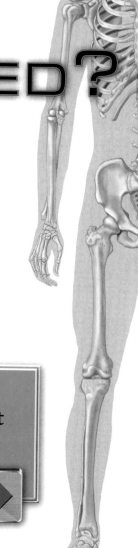

All of the body's bones and the **tissues** that connect them make up the skeletal system. Bones are held together by strips of tissue called ligaments.

In between the bones is a cushion made of cartilage, which is strong but flexible. Cartilage

There are several different kinds of cartilage in the body. One important role of cartilage is to protect bones that come together in joints.

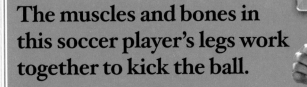

The muscles and bones in this soccer player's legs work together to kick the ball.

keeps bones from grinding against each other. Joints are structures that hold together two or more bones. Joints give the bones support and allow the skeleton to move.

Bones are connected to muscles by tendons, another kind of tough cord. Bones work with muscles to make the body move. In order to move, the brain sends a signal to the muscles. The muscles then pull or push on the bone.

Tissues are groups of cells in the body of a living thing that all carry out the same job.

TYPES OF BONES

There are four types of bones in the human body. Leg and arm bones are examples of long bones. They look like tubes with two bumps at each end. Long bones help the body move. Short bones are found in the ankles and wrists. They are cube-shaped and consist mostly of spongy bone.

Each bone has its own name and function.

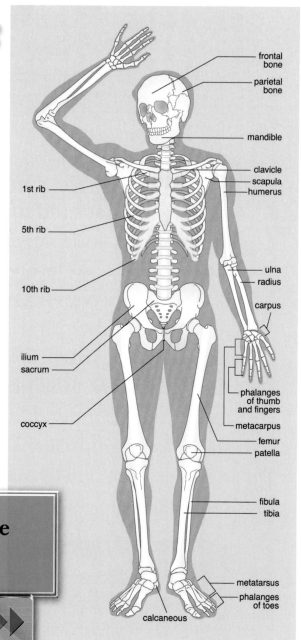

frontal bone

parietal bone

mandible

clavicle
scapula
humerus

1st rib

5th rib

10th rib

ulna
radius

carpus

ilium
sacrum

phalanges of thumb and fingers

metacarpus

coccyx

femur
patella

fibula
tibia

metatarsus
phalanges of toes

calcaneous

THINK ABOUT IT

Feel on your body for the bones mentioned in this section. Can you feel the shapes described here?

The bones in the skull and rib cage are flat bones. They are often thinner than other bones. They protect important organs from damage. Irregular bones don't have any particular shape. They are each unique. They include the upper and lower jawbones and the bones in the spine.

The short bones in these runners' wrists and ankles help them push off to start.

Focus On: The Spine

One interesting group of bones makes up the spine. The spine is easy to find. It runs up and down your back. You can feel its bumpy shape through your skin. The spine helps you stand upright.

The spine is made up of 33 vertebrae. Most of the vertebrae are ring shaped.

anterior view | right lateral view | posterior view

cervical vertebrae (C1–C7)

Atlas (C1)
Axis (C2)
C7
T1

thoracic vertebrae (T1–T12)

T12
L1

lumbar vertebrae (L1–L5)

L5

sacrum (S1–S5)

coccyx

Doctors number vertebrae to make it easier to locate and describe injuries.

Between most of them is a disk of cartilage. There are several groups of vertebrae that do different jobs. At the top of the spine, the cervical vertebrae support the head. Underneath that, the thoracic vertebrae are attached to the ribs, which protect the heart and lungs. Toward the bottom of the spine are the lumbar vertebrae. These provide strength and balance.

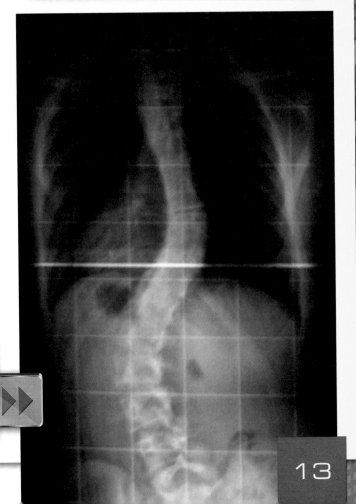

THINK ABOUT IT

Vertebrae are the bones that make up the spine. A single one of these bones is called a vertebra.

This X-ray reveals an abnormal curve in the spine.

Focus On: The Hand

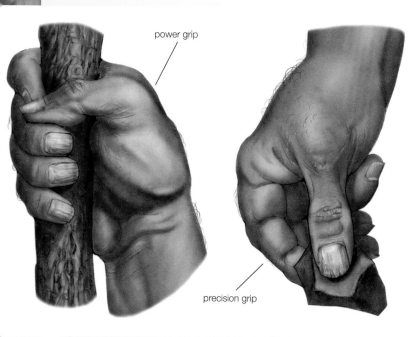

power grip

precision grip

The hand's many small bones allow it to do a variety of tasks.

Human hands are complex. The bones in the hand are connected in ways that let you grip, push, and pull objects.

There are 27 bones in each hand. Each finger has three, and the thumb has two. This group is called the phalanges. The palm has five bones. They are the metacarpals. All of

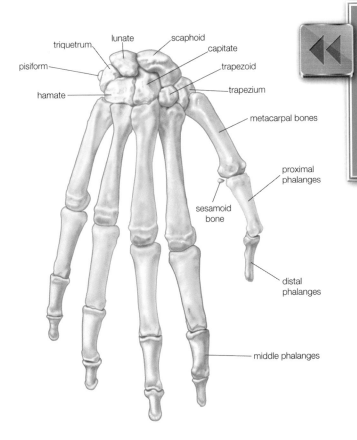

triquetrum
lunate
scaphoid
capitate
pisiform
trapezoid
hamate
trapezium
metacarpal bones
proximal phalanges
sesamoid bone
distal phalanges
middle phalanges

The hand is made of a combination of short and long bones.

these are long bones, which means that they are longer than they are wide. They are connected by joints.

In the wrist, there are eight short bones. These are called carpal bones. Along with four joints, the carpal bones allow your hand to bend and twist.

COMPARE AND CONTRAST

What can your hands do that another animal's paws, claws, or hooves cannot do?

FOCUS ON: THE SKULL

The hard bones in your head make up the skull. The skull acts like a shell for your brain and protects it from injury. It also gives your face its shape.

The cranium, on the top and back of your head, covers your brain. It feels like one piece, but it is actually made up of several bones that are joined together. A baby's cranium has spaces between these bones.

The shape of your skull determines what your face looks like.

Front View

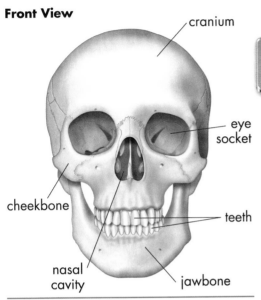

cranium

eye socket

cheekbone

teeth

nasal cavity

jawbone

Side View

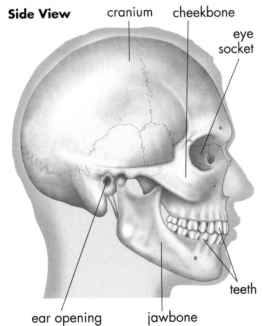

cranium

cheekbone

eye socket

ear opening

jawbone

teeth

The skull is made up mainly of flat bones and irregular bones.

As a baby grows, his or her bones meet up at joints that do not move.

The rest of the skull makes up your face. There are holes that support and protect your eyes and an opening that allows air to come through your nose. There is also a hole for the spinal cord to connect to your brain.

THINK ABOUT IT

How can you protect your skull from injury?

17

Keeping Bones Healthy

There are several ways to keep your bones healthy. The first is to eat foods that have the vitamins and minerals that help build bone. Those foods include milk and other dairy products, leafy green vegetables such as spinach and kale, and some fish.

Exercise also helps make your bones strong. It is good for your muscles and your overall health as well. However,

Having two to three servings of calcium-rich food daily is important for bone health.

COMPARE AND CONTRAST

Think about the types of protective gear a football player and a baseball player wear. Why are they different?

it is important to protect your bones while you are taking part in physical activities. Wearing protective gear like helmets or shin guards while playing sports will give your bones extra protection.

Football players must protect their bones with helmets and padding.

How Do We See Bones?

X-rays can reveal breaks and other injuries.

If there is a problem with one of your bones, a doctor may need to see the bone. The most common way for a doctor to view bones is to use an X-ray machine. X-rays are powerful waves of energy. These rays can go through some material that light cannot go through. To see the bones inside a body, the rays are sent through the body. The X-rays pass through the skin and soft tissues, such as muscle. But hard body parts, such as bones, block the X-rays. Special film captures the image made by the X-rays.

Sometimes, an X-ray picture is not clear enough. In that case, a doctor might order other types of tests that give a clearer image. These tests take longer but can give a doctor more information.

THINK ABOUT IT

Can you think of other uses for an X-ray machine?

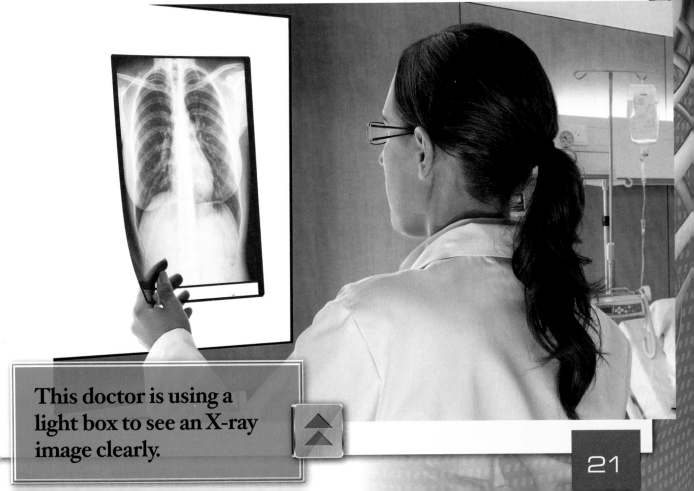

This doctor is using a light box to see an X-ray image clearly.

Breaking a Bone

Even if you eat healthy food and are careful with your body, you might get hurt. Fractures, or broken bones, happen when too much pressure is placed on a bone.

When a bone breaks all the way through but stays under the skin, it is a simple fracture. When a bone breaks and pokes through the skin, it is called a compound fracture.

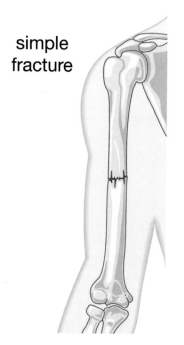
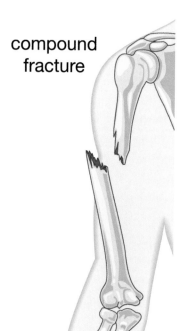

simple fracture

compound fracture

© 2014 Encyclopædia Britannica, Inc.

Some bone breaks are more severe than others.

Doctors use X-rays to see what kind of fracture a patient has. The doctor then sets the bone back in place, sometimes using metal pins, and usually puts a cast over it. A cast can be made of plaster, fiberglass, or plastic. A cast protects the broken bone and keeps it still so it can heal.

THINK ABOUT IT
Which type of fracture would take longer to heal?

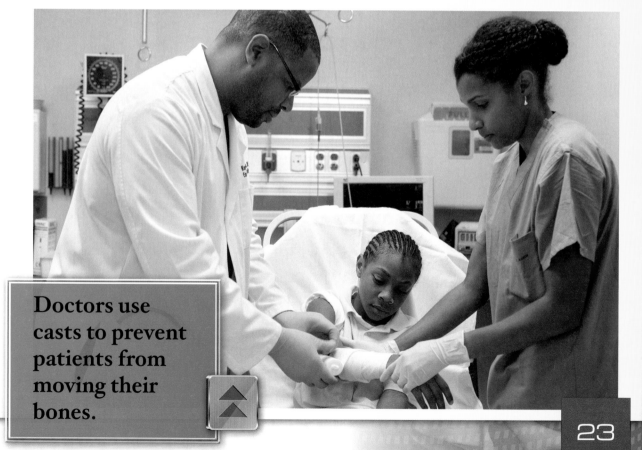

Doctors use casts to prevent patients from moving their bones.

BONE DISEASES

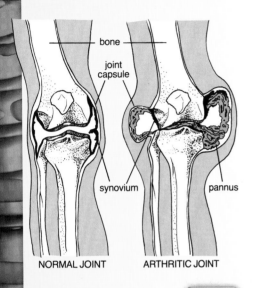

bone
joint capsule
synovium
pannus

NORMAL JOINT   ARTHRITIC JOINT

In some cases, the swelling of an arthritic joint is visible outside of the body.

Like other parts of the body, bones get diseases. Most of the diseases affect older adults. Keeping good health habits when you are young can prevent you from developing some bone diseases.

Arthritis is a disease of the joints, where bones meet. It causes painful swelling. People with arthritis in their hands and wrists have a hard time holding or squeezing things.

Leukemia is a blood cancer that can occur in the bone marrow. The white blood cells of people with leukemia do not work correctly. This makes it

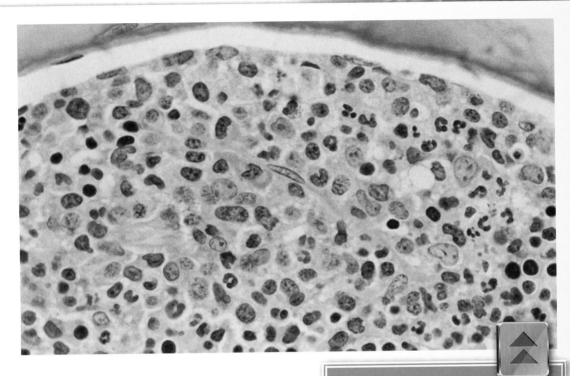

hard for their bodies to fight infections.

After about age 40, people begin to lose some of the material in their bones. If they lose too much, their bones may break easily. Low bone **density** is sometimes caused by poor diet and lack of exercise.

This is a magnified image of the bone marrow of a person with leukemia.

Density means how tightly packed matter is.

Bone Replacement

Bones can sometimes heal themselves by creating new tissue. Special cells start making new bone by building a structure of protein. Blood brings in calcium, which sticks to the protein structure. The calcium builds up and hardens, creating the bone's structure. Sometimes, however, bones cannot heal themselves. Joints can wear out over time, or disease can wear away at bones. Scientists therefore have come up with several ways to replace bones.

Surgeons can replace hips, knees, shoulders, and many other joints and bones. The replacements

This doctor holds a ceramic hip joint.

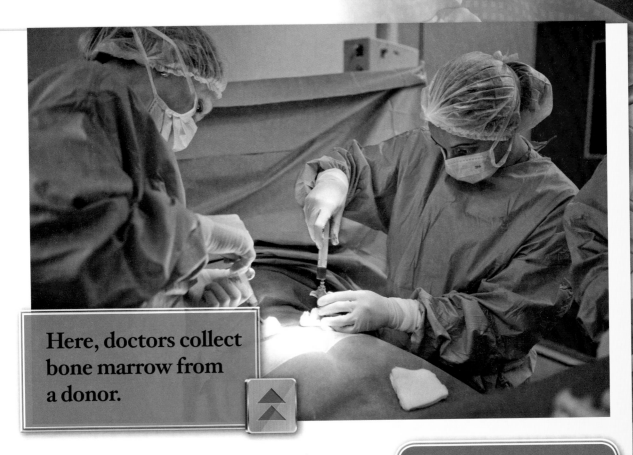

Here, doctors collect bone marrow from a donor.

are usually made of metals, ceramics, and plastics.

Bone marrow creates blood cells for our bodies, so it is important for it to stay healthy. When it becomes diseased, doctors may perform a bone marrow transplant.

THINK ABOUT IT

Why would family members make the best bone marrow donors?

Scientists around the world are experimenting with new ways to create better **artificial** bones. Rattan, a type of wood, has been used to replace bones in animals after it has been treated with chemicals and heated. Other scientists are using forms of plastic to create molds for metal replacement bones.

Another exciting new tool for doctors is 3-D printing. A 3-D printer works like a computer printer, but instead of printing a flat page, it uses plastics

Titanium and steel parts are often used to strengthen or replace bones.

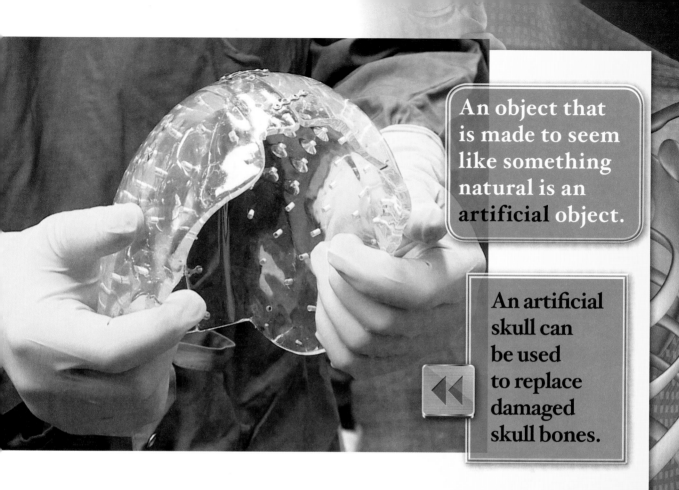

An object that is made to seem like something natural is an artificial object.

An artificial skull can be used to replace damaged skull bones.

and other substances to create an object from exact measurements. The object can be placed in the body, where bone cells can attach to it and grow new bone. This means that, in the future, a doctor could create a whole new bone for a person that would fit perfectly.

GLOSSARY

bone marrow A soft substance that fills the bones of people and animals.

cancer A serious disease caused by cells that are not normal and that can spread to one or many parts of the body.

cartilage Strong, flexible material found between bones.

cells The smallest units of living matter that can exist by themselves.

complex Made of many parts.

digit A finger or toe.

fractures Breaks.

injury Harm or damage.

irregular Not having a standard size or shape.

joints Places where bones meet.

ligament Tissue that holds bones in place, like a rubber band.

membrane A thin, protective cover.

minerals Substances (such as iron or zinc) that occur naturally in certain foods and are important for good health.

muscles Body tissue that can contract and produce movement.

nutrients Natural substances that the body needs to function.

organs Body parts that have a particular job.

protein A substance found in foods (such as meat, milk, eggs, and beans) that is an important part of the human diet.

skeletal system The collection of bones inside the body.

tendons Bands that connect muscles to bones.

transplant Taking something from one place and putting it in another place.

X-ray A powerful wave of energy; a picture taken with radiation.

FOR MORE INFORMATION

Books

Arnold, Caroline. *Your Skeletal System*. Minneapolis, MN: Lerner Publications, 2012.

Baines, Rebecca. *The Bones You Own: A Book About the Bones in Your Body*. Washington, D.C.: National Geographic, 2009.

Houghton, Gillian. *Bones: The Skeletal System*. New York, NY: PowerKids Press, 2007.

Jenkins, Steve. *Bones: Skeletons and How They Work*. New York, NY: Scholastic Press, 2010.

Rotnor, Shelly. *Body Bones*. New York, NY: Holiday House, 2014.

Websites

Because of the changing nature of Internet links, Rosen Publishing has developed an online list of websites related to the subject of this book. This site is updated regularly. Please use this link to access the list:

http://www.rosenlinks.com/LFO/Bones

INDEX